Best of
Blueberries

Best of
Blueberries

R. Marilyn Schmidt

KFR
Communications, LLC

Best of Blueberries

First edition copyright © 1993, 2003 by R. Marilyn Schmidt
Published by Pine Barrens Press, a division of
Barnegat Light Press, Chatsworth, NJ

Second edition copyright © 2012 by R. Marilyn Schmidt
Cover art copyright © by Andrew Gioulis
Book design by KFR Communications

Published by: KFR Communications, LLC
          148 Hawkin Rd
          New Egypt, NJ 08533

Publisher's Note: The author and publisher have taken
care in preparation of this book but make no expressed or
implied warranty of any kind and assume no responsibility
for errors or omissions. No liability is assumed for inciden-
tal or consequential damages in connection with or arising
out of the use of the information contained herein.

ISBN-10: 0982895968
ISBN-13: 978-0-9828959-6-2

Printed in the United States of America

www.kfrcommunications.com

This book replaces our publications, *All About Blueberries* and *The Best of Blueberries*.

Because of many requests, information about growing blueberries and using them in landscaping is included.

Most of our old favorite recipes are included plus some new ones. Hope you enjoy!

Contents

INTRODUCTION

Growing blueberries is a major industry in the United States. In New Jersey alone the annual value surpasses 108 million dollars. Over twenty varieties of blueberries are grown. The best known is "Blue Crop."

Several varieties of blueberries are available in the marketplace. Three major types are cultivated. In the middle Atlantic area, high bush blueberries (*Vaccinium corymbosum*) are popular. In the south, rabbiteye blueberries (*Vaccinium ashei*) are grown. In Maine and Nova Scotia, wild blueberries or low bush blueberries (*Vaccinium angustifolium, V. lamarkii*) are found in abundance.

The huckleberry (*Gaylussacia sp*), a cousin to the highbush blueberry, is found in the middle Atlantic area and is distinguished by its 10 large seeds; blueberries have many, small soft seeds.

Highbush Blueberries

Although a native American fruit, the cultivated highbush blueberry was developed in the early 1900s. These berries, grown in New Jersey, Michigan, Oregon, Washington, and British Columbia, will reach up to 15 feet in height and have rather specific cultural requirements. Highbush blueberries require a soil pH of 4.5 to 5.2. Addition of sulfur or aluminum sulfate to the soil will decrease the pH to this range

Additionally, blueberries require a well-drained soil with a high concentration of organic matter such as peat moss. Two cultivars are required for pollination. Moisture must be plentiful for the growing season.

Highbush blueberries require for the most part, a lengthy cold period before they will blossom. Many varieties, therefore, cannot be grown south of North Carolina. Sunbelt gardeners can grow rabbiteye blueberries which need only 200 to 500 hours of temperatures below 32°F and 45°F.

Rabbiteye Blueberries

Like highbush blueberries, rabbiteye or southern blueberries, need moist soil with a pH between 4.0 and 5.0 and plenty of nitrogen. Peat moss aids in retaining moisture and provides needed organic matter. Rabbiteye blueberries are not self-pollinating; consequently, a grower must have at least two different varieties. In the south with the longer growing season, the berries need a bit more nitrogen than the highbush plants.

In general, growers of rabbiteyes apply 12-4-8 fertilizer from April to September, varying the amount according to the plant's size. For example, in the first season after transplanting, one ounce of fertilizer is applied to each plant four to six times during the season; during the second year, this amount is doubled; from the third year on, plants can handle three to four ounces three to six times during the season.

In the south, keeping plants moist is crucial. Bushes need about one inch of water per week in the summer. Pine bark chips are a good mulch to keep roots cool, control weeds, and hold moisture in the sandy soil. Rabbiteyes need little pruning, even less than highbush blueberries.

Since these plants can reach 15 feet in height, it is advantageous to prune the tops so the fruit can be reached. The oldest wood can be pruned each year after the plants are three years old. This allows light to reach the center of the plants. A well tended bush will produce as much as 35 pounds a year over a period of up to six weeks. Few diseases affect rabbiteyes; mummy-berry, a fungal infection, is sometimes a problem.

Wild (Low Bush) Blueberries
Harvested primarily in Maine, these little berries are preferred by bakers since they keep their shape and are said to be sweeter, tastier, and juicer than other blueberries. Maine grows 98% of America's wild blueberry crop. In the Pine Barrens of New Jersey these berries may be found; they are not grown commercially here. Wild blueberries make an excellent ground cover in the garden.

The wild blueberry is a low bush plant which thrives in poor, sandy soil where other plants refuse to grow. In fact, wild blueberries are difficult to eradicate. Following a fire, it is often the first plant to regrow. Wild blueberries are difficult to transplant; they are only to be tended.

Wild blueberries are eaten fresh and can be frozen or sun dried. Native Americans pounded berries into their venison as a preservative; they used the juice as a cough medicine and the tea as a relaxant to ease the pain of childbirth.

Wild blueberries are harvested using a blueberry rake. This rake, unchanged since 1882, looks like a dust pan with high sides, an inverted handle, and a long-toothed comb bottom. The raker faces uphill and takes short strokes away from the body, so the stripped berries fall into the rake's reservoir. A field is only harvested every other year, a practice handed down from the Indians. When the harvest is over, the fields harvested will be raked, then covered with hay. In the early spring, the fields will be burned as the natives did. This kills weeds and insect larvae, and also prunes the berries.

In early May, the dark fields turn spring green. The plants soon set buds for next year's harvest. The fields not harvested begin turning ivory and pink with blueberry blossoms. Then bee hives are brought in, one to an acre. Honey bees traditionally pollinate the berries. If weather is wet or foggy, the bees won't work, and the crop is diminished.

Since the early 1980s, new herbicides have changed the growing procedure. Yield is increased with the elimination of undesirable plants. Burning is no longer necessary. New harvesting equipment to mechanically harvest the crop has been developed. Procedures and equipment change as the demand for wild blueberries increases.

Wild blueberries are also harvested in Canada and Nova Scotia, but Maine remains the major producer.

Landscaping with Blueberries
Blueberry bushes are underused and underappreciated ornamental plants. In the fall, the green leaves turn a beautiful bright red. In the spring, the bushes are covered with pink and white flowers. In summer the bushes provide delicious fruit and dark green folliage.

The plants vary in height but will grow as tall as eight feet. These bushes make great hedges; their fairly dense twiggy growth makes a good barrier without looking too tangled. Bushes can be clipped into a formal angular hedge; this, however, sacrifices fruit. Blueberry plants can be used to line walks, edge patios or property lines to provide privacy, or serve as a border or backdrop for flower beds.

Highbush blueberries will grow in Zones 5 to 7; in zones 3 to 4, low bush blueberries will grow best. In zones 8 to 10, heat-tolerant southern high bush types grow and in zones 7 to 9, rabbiteye blueberries are preferred.

Soil requirements for all blueberries are a pH of from 4.5 to 5.2. To obtain this add sulfur or aluminum sulfate to the soil. Blueberries require well-drained soil. At least two cultivars are needed for cross pollination.

When planting blueberries, add organic matter into the

planting hole, three inches of peat, to a depth of 18 inches before planting. Do not substitute sawdust, hay, or compost instead of peat. Serious nitrogen problems may result after the materials start to decompose.

Two-year plants, 18 to 24 inches high, should be planted in the spring before growth begins. One can also plant later in the fall after first frost. Do not fertilize plants the first year. Mulch plants with an organic mulch such as pine needles or rotted wood chips over the root zone up to 4 inches across. Make the mulch 4 to 6 inches deep. Leave a three inch circle clear around the plant stem to protect the bark from heat during mulch decomposition. Mulch should last two years.

Blueberry plants should be fertilized the second year after planting. Use fertilizer with ammonia as primary source of nitrogen, such as ammonium sulfate. As the bushes grow, increase the fertilizer. Soil should be kept moist. Blueberry plants do not have root hairs and consequently can't absorb moisture efficiently. Fruit yields will increase with adequate irrigation. Provide one to two inches of water every 10 days.

Different varieties of berries yield at different times: early fruiters include Collins, Earliblue, and Bluetta; midseason fruiters include Jersey, Blue Crop, Berkeley, and Blueray; late season fruiters include Coville and Darrow. Many other varieties are available. Consult your local agricultural agent or plant catalogs for this information.

Blueberries seldom experience major problems with insects and disease. Birds, however, are a problem. Robins, quail, and brown thrashers or thrushes are fond of blueberries. It may be necessary to protect fruit with netting.

Yellowing of foliage is due to iron chlorosis and nitrogen deficiency. With iron chlorosis, areas between veins turn yellow. With nitrogen deficiency, foliage is yellow all over. Leaf scorch may also occur. Leaf edges turn brown and leaves roll inward. This may be due to environmental conditions or to low moisture.

Blueberries bear fruit on wood of the previous season. The best fruits come on the most vigorous wood. At planting time, remove 1/4 to 1/3 of the top of the plant. The first two years, remove blossoms from plants. The third year and afterwards, allow fruiting.

On mature bushes prune out old canes every year; plants should never have canes more than 4 or 5 years old. Keep the height below 6 feet for easy harvesting. Properly pruned and well-nourished plants should live and produce berries for many years. Feed and water in August and September as fruit buds form for next year.

Harvest blueberries when they are deep blue or black with a frosted appearance. Blueberries may be eaten fresh, cooked, frozen, or dried.

Drying Blueberries

Drying blueberries goes back to Indian tradition. Drying helps recapture some of the flavor intensity of their wild relatives. Drying is easy. Just spread berries in a single layer on baking sheets. Place in a sunny spot for 4 or 5 days, or bake in a very low oven (200°F) for 4 or 5 hours. Berries fully dried will keep indefinitely in a plastic bag or glass jar. Dried berries plump up in any liquid.

Freezing Blueberries

Unwashed, fresh blueberries can be stored in plastic containers or bags in the freezer. Glass jars that seal tightly are great; the berries will last for years. Wash berries before using.

Another method is to wash the berries and dry them on paper towels before freezing. Store in plastic containers. Berries are then ready to eat from the container or use in any dishes.

BLUEBERRY ROLY-POLY *Serves 6 to 8*

3/4 cup sugar

1/4 cup flour

1/8 teaspoon salt

1 tablespoon lemon juice

1 quart blueberries, washed, dried

Biscuit Dough

3 cups flour

6 tablespoons butter, cold

1/2 teaspoon salt

3 teaspoons baking powder

1 cup milk

2 tablespoons butter, melted

2 tablespoons sugar

1/2 teaspoon cinnamon, ground

Optional cream, whipped

Heat oven to 425°F. Grease and flour a cookie sheet. Set aside.

In a large bowl, combine 3/4 cup sugar, flour, salt, lemon juice, and 3-1/2 cups blueberries. Mix gently; set aside.

Biscuit Dough

In a medium bowl sift together the flour, salt, and baking powder. With a pastry blender, cut butter into flour mixture until it resembles coarse meal. With a fork stir in milk until dough holds together. Roll on a floured board to form a 16x9-inch rectangle. Brush thoroughly with melted butter.

In a small bowl, combine sugar and cinnamon; mix together.

Sprinkle over Biscuit Dough.

Spread blueberry mixture down center of dough; roll up and shape in a ring. Place on greased cookie sheet. Pinch ends together. With scissors, make cuts in ring at 2-inch intervals, cutting not quite to center.

Bake in 425°F oven for 25 to 30 minutes. Spoon reserved berries into center of ring; top with whipped cream, if desired.

Serve while still warm.

BLUEBERRY COFFEE CAKE *Serves 8*

1 cup sugar
1 teaspoon cinnamon, ground
1-3/4 cups flour
2 teaspoons baking powder
1/4 teaspoon cardamon
5 tablespoons butter
1egg
1/2 cup milk
1 cup blueberries

In a small bowl, combine 1 tablespoon sugar and cinnamon; set aside.

Heat oven to 375°F. Grease and flour an 8-inch square pan. Set aside.

In a medium bowl, combine remaining sugar, flour, baking powder, and cardamon. Cut in butter until mixture resembles cornmeal.

In a small bowl, beat egg with milk; add to batter. Stir until just combined. Stir in blueberries.

Spoon batter into prepared pan. Sprinkle sugar-cinnamon mixture over top. Bake in 375°F oven for 20 to 25 minutes, or until a toothpick inserted in center of cake comes out clean. Cool on a rack. Serve warm or at room temperature.

BLUEBERRY SHORTCAKE *Serves 6 to 8*

Sponge cake

3/4 cup flour

1/4 cup cornstarch

1 teaspoon baking powder

Pinch salt

4 eggs, large

3/4 cup sugar

1 lemon, small, grated zest

1/2 teaspoon vanilla

Filling

4 cups blueberries, washed, dried

to taste sugar

Garnish cream, whipped

Heat oven to 350°F. Grease and flour a 9-inch square cake pan. Set aside.

Place berries in a large bowl. Sprinkle with sugar. Crush berries lightly and allow to stand for 1 to 2 hours until juicy. Reserve a few whole berries for garnishing cake.

Sponge Cake

In a medium bowl, combine flour, cornstarch, baking powder, and salt. Set aside.

In a large bowl, beat eggs, sugar, and lemon zest until very thick, pale yellow, and at least double in volume, about 5 minutes. Fold in vanilla and melted butter; mix until blended.

Quickly fold in dry ingredients, adding about 1/4 cup at a time. When ingredients are thoroughly blended together, pour batter into cake pan.

Bake until cake is puffed, lightly golden, and center springs back when pressed lightly, about 35 minutes. Remove cake from oven. Cool thoroughly on a rack. When cool, remove from pan and split cake into two layers. Fill bottom layer with fruit, replace top layer and decorate with whipped cream and whole berries.

BLUEBERRY GINGERBREAD *Makes a 9x13 inch cake*

1 cup butter, room temperature

1/2 cup honey

1/2 cup molasses

4 eggs

3 cups flour

1 teaspoon baking powder

1 teaspoon baking soda

2 teaspoons ginger, ground

1 teaspoon cinnamon, ground

1/4 teaspoon cloves, ground

1/4 teaspoon nutmeg, ground

1-1/4 cups blueberries, washed, dried

1 cup water, boiling

Heat oven to 350°F. Butter and flour a 9x13-inch baking pan. Set aside.

In a large bowl, cream butter for 2 minutes; add honey and molasses. Cream mixture 2 minutes longer. Beat in eggs, one at a time.

In another bowl combine flour, baking powder, baking soda, ginger, cinnamon, cloves, and nutmeg; mix until well combined. Remove 1/4 cup of mixture and toss with blueberries.
Stir flour mixture into butter-egg mixture alternately with boiling water. Stir only until smooth, or gingerbread will

be tough. Stir in floured-blueberries. Pour batter into baking pan. Bake in 350°F oven for about 40 minutes, or until cooked through. Test with a toothpick. Cool before serving.

BLUEBERRY GRUNT   *Serves 6*

3 cups blueberries, washed, dried

2 tablespoons lemon juice, fresh

1/2 cup sugar

1/4 teaspoon cinnamon, ground

1/8 teaspoon nutmeg, ground

Topping

1 cup flour

2 tablespoons sugar

1-1/2 teaspoons baking powder

1/4 teaspoon salt

1/4 cup butter

1/2 cup milk

1 egg, beaten

Heat oven to 375°F.

In an 8-inch square baking dish, combine blueberries, lemon juice, sugar, cinnamon, and nutmeg. Mix well. Bake 5 minutes; remove from oven. Increase oven temperature to 425°F.

Topping

In a medium bowl, combine flour, sugar, baking powder, and salt. With pastry blender cut in butter.

In a small bowl mix well egg and milk. Stir into dry ingredients just until moistened. Spread batter over hot berries. Bake 20 minutes, or until nicely browned. Serve warm!

BLUEBERRY SOUR-CREAM CAKE *Serves 4 to 8*

3 cups blueberries, washed, dried

2 cups flour

1/4 pound butter

1-1/2 cups sugar

2 eggs, beaten

1 cup sour cream

1 lemon rind, grated

1 tablespoon baking powder

2 teaspoons cinnamon, ground

1 teaspoon cloves, ground

1/2 teaspoon salt

Heat oven to 350°F. Grease and flour a bundt pan.

In a large bowl, coat berries with 1/3 cup flour; set aside.

In a large bowl, cream butter and sugar; beat in eggs and sour cream. Add lemon rind.

In another bowl, combine flour, baking powder, cinnamon, cloves, and salt; mix well. Fold this mixture into egg batter. Fold in coated blueberries.

Pour batter into prepared pan and bake at 350°F for 1 to 1-2 hours, or until fork comes out clean. Cool 10 minutes in pan, then turn onto cake rack. When cake is cool, sprinkle with powdered sugar.

BLUEBERRY UPSIDE-DOWN CAKE   *Serves 6*

1-1/2 cups blueberries, washed, dried

6 tablespoons brown sugar, light, packed firm

1 cup flour, unbleached

1-1/2 teaspoons baking powder

1/4 teaspoon salt

1/2 pound butter

1/2 cup sugar

1 teaspoon vanilla

1 egg, large

1/4 cup milk

As needed cream, whipped

Heat oven to 400°F.

Butter six 6-ounce custard cups. Divide berries among these cups. Crumble 1 tablespoon brown sugar over berries in each cup.

On wax paper, stir together flour, baking powder, and salt.

In medium bowl, cream butter, sugar, and vanilla; add egg and beat to blend. Stir in flour mixture in two additions, alternately with milk, mixing only until smooth. Drop over berries.

Bake in 400°F oven until cake tester inserted in center comes out free of batter, about 20 minutes. Let stand on wire rack for 5 minutes. Loosen edges and turn out onto individual plates. Serve hot topped with whipped cream.

BLUEBERRY-CARROT CAKE   *Serves 8 to 10*

2 cups flour, unbleached

2 teaspoons baking powder

2 teaspoons cinnamon, ground

1 teaspoon baking soda

1 teaspoon salt

1 cup sugar

1/2 cup brown sugar, light, packed firm

4 eggs, large

1 cup corn oil

4 carrots, medium, peeled, grated coarse

2 cups blueberries, washed, dried

1 cup walnuts, chopped coarse

As needed cream, whipped, unsweetened

Heat oven to 350°F. Grease and flour a 10-cup bundt pan.

In medium bowl, combine flour, baking powder, cinnamon, baking soda, and salt. Mix well.

In a large bowl, combine both sugars. Add eggs, one at a time, whisking until smooth. Whisk in oil. Stir in carrots, blueberries, and walnuts. Add dry ingredients and fold until just blended; do not overmix. This batter will be quite thick.

Spoon batter into bundt pan. Bake in 350°F oven about 1 hour, until cake begins to pull away from sides of pan and tester inserted in center comes out clean. Cool cake in pan on rack 20 minutes. Invert onto plate. Cool completely. Serve with a dollop of unsweetened whipped cream and fresh berries. Delicious!

OLD-FASHIONED BLUEBERRY CAKE *Serves 10 to 12*

2 tablespoons sugar

2/3 cup water

2 cups blueberries, washed, dried

1/2 pound butter

2 cups sugar

4 eggs, beaten

1 teaspoon cinnamon, ground

1 teaspoon nutmeg, ground

1 teaspoon cloves, ground

1 teaspoon salt

3 cups flour

1 cup raisins, golden

1 cup apricot preserves

2 teaspoons baking soda

1/2 cup buttermilk

Garnish confectioners sugar

Heat oven to 350°F. Grease and flour 3 8-inch round pans.

In medium bowl, combine blueberries with 2 tablespoons sugar and water. Allow to stand 30 minutes.

In a large bowl, cream butter and sugar until light and fluffy. Add eggs, cinnamon, nutmeg, cloves, salt, blueberry mixture, flour, raisins, and preserves. Beat until well blended. Dissolve baking soda in buttermilk and add to batter. Mix well but do not overmix.

Pour batter into cake pans. Bake in 350°F oven for 25 to 35 minutes, or until cake tester inserted in center comes out clean. Remove cakes from pans; cool on wire racks. Sprinkle with confectioners sugar between layers and on top of cake.

This cake can also be baked in 2 4x8-inch loaf pans in 350°F oven for 50 to 60 minutes.

BLUEBERRY BOTTOM CAKE *Serves 6 to 8*

Topping
2 tablespoons sugar

1/8 teaspoon mace, ground

1/4 teaspoon lemon peel, grated

1 tablespoon butter, room temperature

Berries
1 pint blueberries, washed, dried

1/2 cup sugar

1 tablespoon flour

2 teaspoons lemon peel, grated

1/8 teaspoon mace, ground

2 tablespoons butter, unsalted

Cake
1-1/3 cups flour

3/4 teaspoon baking powder

3/4 teaspoon baking soda

1/4 teaspoon mace, ground

1/8 teaspoon salt

6 tablespoons butter, room temperature

1/2 cup sugar

2 eggs, room temperature

1-1/2 teaspoons lemon peel, grated

1/2 teaspoon vanilla

2/3 cup sour cream
Garnish confectioners sugar
Optional vanilla ice cream

Heat oven to 350°F. Butter a 2-quart baking dish with 2-inch sides. Set aside.

Topping
In small bowl, combine all ingredients and mix until crumbly. Set aside.

Berries
In baking dish combine blueberries, sugar, flour, lemon peel, and mace. Cut butter over surface. Bake 10 minutes.

Cake
In medium bowl, sift flour, baking powder, baking soda, mace, and salt.

In another bowl, with an electric mixer, cream butter. Add sugar and beat until light and fluffy. Beat in eggs, one at a time.

Blend in lemon peel and vanilla. Mix dry ingredients alternately with sour cream, beginning and ending with dry. Drop batter by large spoonfuls atop berries. Spread to sides of dish. Dot with topping.

Bake in 350°F oven for about 40 minutes, or until tester inserted in center of cake comes out clean. Cool on rack at least 25 minutes. Sprinkle with confectioners sugar. Serve warm or at room temperature with ice cream.

BLUEBERRY PECAN COFFEE CAKE   *Serves 16*

Pecan Topping
1/2 cup butter

1 cup flour

1/2 cup pecans, chopped

3/4 cup sugar

1 tablespoon lemon peel, grated

Cake
1/2 cup butter

3/4 cup sugar

1-1/4 cups flour

2 teaspoons baking powder

2 teaspoons lemon peel, grated

1/4 teaspoon salt

4 eggs

1 pint blueberries, washed, dried

Heat oven to 325°F. Grease and flour a 13x9-inch baking dish.

Topping
In small saucepan over medium heat, melt butter; remove saucepan from heat. Stir in flour, pecans, sugar, and lemon peel; mix to form soft dough. Set aside.

Cake

In large bowl, cream butter and sugar until light and fluffy. Add flour, baking powder, lemon peel, salt, and eggs; beat just until blended, occasionally scraping bowl with rubber spatula. Beat until smooth. Spread batter evenly in baking dish. Top with blueberries.

Pinch pecan topping into small pieces; scatter over batter. Bake in 325°F oven for 45 minutes, or until golden and toothpick inserted in center comes out clean. Serve warm. Or, cool coffee cake completely on wire rack to serve cold.

PORTED BLUEBERRY CRISP   *Serves 6 to 8*

4 cups blueberries, washed, dried

1/4 cup Ruby Port

3/4 cup flour

3/4 cup brown sugar, light, packed firm

1/2 cup butter, cold, cut into bits

Heat oven to 375°F. Butter well a shallow 1-quart glass baking dish.

In baking dish combine blueberries and port. Set aside.

In a bowl combine flour, brown sugar, and butter. Blend mixture until it resembles meal. Sprinkle mixture evenly over blueberries.

Bake in 375°F oven for 30 to 40 minutes, or until top is golden. Serve the crisp warm with vanilla ice cream, if desired.

BLUEBERRY KUCHEN

2 cups flour

2 teaspoons baking powder

1/2 teaspoon salt

1/4 cup butter

3/4 cup sugar

1 egg, large

1/2 cup milk

2 cups blueberries, washed, dried

Streusel Topping

1/2 cup brown sugar, light, packed firm

3 tablespoons flour, unbleached

2 teaspoons cinnamon

3 tablespoons butter

1/2 cup walnuts, chopped fine

Heat oven to 375°F. Butter and flour a 9-inch spring form pan. Set aside.

On wax paper or in a bowl thoroughly combine baking powder, flour, and salt.

In large bowl, cream butter and sugar; beat in egg until blended. Add flour mixture and milk; stir just until dry ingredients are moistened. Fold in blueberries. Turn batter into pan and sprinkle with Streusel Topping.

Bake in 375°F oven until cake tester inserted in center comes out clean, 45 to 50 minutes. If topping begins to get very brown, cover loosely with aluminum foil.

Cool cake on wire rack for 5 minutes. Loosen edges; remove spring form band. Serve warm.

Streusel Topping
In medium bowl, stir together brown sugar, flour, cinnamon, and butter. With pastry blender cut in butter until fine particles form. Stir in walnuts. Set aside.

Sprinkle over top of cake batter before baking.

BLUEBERRY CRISP   *Serves 4 to 6*
4 cups blueberries, washed, drained

1/3 cup sugar

2 teaspoons lemon juice

4 tablespoons butter

1/3 cup sugar, brown, light

1/3 cup flour

3/4 cup quick cooking oats

Heat oven to 375°F. Grease a deep 1-quart baking dish.

In baking dish, place blueberries; sprinkle with sugar and lemon juice. Set aside.

In a small bowl, cream butter and brown sugar; add flour

and oats. Mix well. Spread mixture over blueberries. Bake in 375°F oven for 40 minutes.

Serve warm with whipped cream, if desired.

BLUEBERRY COBBLER   *Serves 4 to 5*

Fruit Mixture

3 cups blueberries, washed, dried

1/2 cup sugar

1/2 teaspoon lemon zest, grated

2 teaspoons lemon juice, fresh

1 teaspoon vanilla

1 tablespoon butter

Cobbler Dough

1 cup flour

2 teaspoons baking powder

1/2 teaspoon salt

1 tablespoon sugar

2 tablespoons butter, cold

1/3 cup cream, whipping

For dusting confectioners sugar

Heat oven to 425°F.

Fruit Mixture

In mixing bowl, toss berries with sugar, lemon zest, lemon juice, and vanilla. Place fruit mixture in 1-quart baking dish. Cut butter into several pieces and scatter over fruit. Set aside.

Cobbler Dough

In a large bowl, combine flour, baking powder, salt, and sugar. Mix well. Cut in butter until mixture resembles coarse meal.

Pour in cream and mix until dough forms a ball. Turn out onto lightly floured surface and roll into shape that is slightly smaller than interior dimensions of baking dish and about 1/4-inch thick. Trim edges and crimp with finger tips.

Place dough over fruit. Dough should be smaller than interior of dish by about 1/4-inch so that steam can escape. Cut several deep slashes in cobbler top so that additional steam can escape.

Bake in 425°F oven for 20 to 25 minutes, or until crust is golden brown and fruit is tender. Cool on rack. Serve warm or at room temperature with confectioners sugar sifted over crust.

BLUEBERRY PANDOWDY   *Serves 6*

5 cups blueberries, washed, dried

2 tablespoons cornstarch

1 teaspoon cinnamon, ground

1/2 teaspoon nutmeg, ground

1/2 cup sugar

1-1/4 cups flour

2 teaspoons baking powder

1/2 teaspoon salt

1 egg, large

1/2 cup milk

1/4 cup butter, room temperature

Optional sugar and nutmeg

Heat oven to 375°F.

In a large bowl, toss berries with cornstarch, cinnamon, nutmeg, and 2 tablespoons sugar.

In medium bowl, combine flour, remaining sugar, baking powder, and salt. Make well in center. Add egg, milk, and butter. Mix until well combined.

In a 1-quart baking dish, place berries. Top with pandowdy batter. If desired, sprinkle with a little sugar and nutmeg. Bake until top is golden, about 35 to 40 minutes. Serve warm.

DOUBLE BLUEBERRY BUCKLE   *Serves 8*

1/4 cup butter

3/4 cup sugar

1 tablespoon lemon juice

1 teaspoon lemon rind, grated

2 cups flour

2 teaspoons baking powder

1/4 teaspoon salt

1/2 cup milk

1 cup blueberries, washed, dried

Blueberry Topping

1/4 cup sugar

1 tablespoon cornstarch

1/8 teaspoon cinnamon, ground

1/4 cup water

1 teaspoon lemon juice

1 cup blueberries, divided

Heat oven to 375°F. Grease and flour a 9-inch square pan.

In a large bowl, cream butter and sugar until light and fluffy. Beat in egg, lemon juice, and lemon rind. Add dry ingredients alternately with milk. Gently fold in blueberries.

Spread dough into pan. Bake for 25 to 35 minutes, or until toothpick inserted in center comes out clean.

In small saucepan over medium heat, combine topping ingredients, reserving 2 cup blueberries. Cook, stirring, until thickened. Spread hot topping over warm cake. Use reserved blueberries for top decoration. Serve warm.

BLUEBERRY AND NECTARINE BUCKLE

Serves 8 to 10

Topping

1/4 cup butter, cold, cut into bits

1/2 cup sugar

1/3 cup flour

1/2 teaspoon cinnamon, ground

1/2 teaspoon nutmeg, grated fresh

If desired cream, whipped

Batter

3/4 cup butter, room temperature

3/4 cup sugar

1 teaspoon vanilla

1/4 teaspoonbaking powder

1-1/3 cups flour

1/2 teaspoon salt

3 eggs, large

2 cups blueberries, washed, dried

2 nectarines, pitted, cut into 1-inch wedges

Heat oven to 350°F. Butter a 10-inch round cake pan. Set aside.

Topping

In small bowl, blend together sugar, butter, flour, cinnamon, and nutmeg until mixture resembles coarse meal. Chill topping while making batter.

Batter

In large bowl, cream together butter and sugar; beat in vanilla.

In small bowl, combine baking powder, flour, and salt. Beat flour mixture into butter mixture alternately with eggs, one at a time, beating well after each addition. Fold in blueberries and nectarines.

Spread batter in cake pan, sprinkle topping evenly, and bake in 350°F oven for 45 to 50 minutes, or until tester comes out clean and topping is crisp and golden. Serve buckle with whipped cream or ice cream, if desired.

EASY BLUEBERRY PIE   *Serves 6 to 8*

1 tablespoon lemon juice, fresh

1/2 cup sugar

2 tablespoons cornstarch

1 quart blueberries, washed, dried

1 9-inch pie crust, baked

In a small saucepan, combine lemon juice, sugar, cornstarch, and 1 pint blueberries. Over low heat, bring mixture to a boil; let boil 3 or 4 minutes, or until thick.

In pie shell, put 1 pint fresh blueberries. Pour cooked berries on top. Serve hot!

DEEP DISH BLUEBERRY-PIE   *Serves 6 to 8*

1 egg white, beaten

2 pie dough crusts (purchased or homemade)

4 cups blueberries, washed, dried

3/4 cup sugar

2-1/2 tablespoons tapioca, quick-cooking

2-1/2 tablespoons lemon rind, grated

1 tablespoon lemon juice

1/4 teaspoon cinnamon

As needed butter

Heat oven to 450°F.

Roll out dough for crust for 9-inch deep pie plate. Brush bottom and sides with egg white.
In a large bowl, combine blueberries, sugar, tapioca, lemon rind, lemon juice, and cinnamon; mix well. Transfer mixture to pie shell, mounding berry mixture slightly in center. Dot filling with butter bits.

Roll out remaining dough and drape over filling. Trim top crust, fold it under bottom crust to seal the pie, and crimp edge decoratively. Make slits in top crust for steam to escape. Brush top crust with milk; chill pie in freezing compartment of refrigerator for 10 minutes, or until dough is firm.

Bake pie on preheated baking sheet on lowest rack at 450°F for 15 minutes; reduce heat to 375°F and bake pie for 35 to 40 minutes more, or until crust is golden and filling is bubbly. Best served warm.

BLUEBERRY WHIPPED CREAM PIE   *Serves 6*

1 9-inch pastry shell, baked, cooled

2 cups blueberries, washed, dried

3/4 cup sugar

1/4 teaspoon salt

2 tablespoons cornstarch

2/3 cup water, boiling

2 tablespoons butter

1-1/2 tablespoons lemon juice, fresh

1/2 pint cream, whipping

2 tablespoons confectioners sugar

In medium saucepan, blend sugar, salt, and cornstarch. Stir in water and 1 cup blueberries. Over low heat, bring mixture to boil; stir gently until mixture becomes thick and clear, 3 to 4 minutes. Cool, until lukewarm, then gently fold in remaining blueberries. Cover and place in refrigerator until cold but not set.

About 1 hour before serving, whip cream until thick. Sift in confectioners sugar and continue beating until stiff. Spread whipped cream over pie shell, leaving cream layer a little higher around edge. Turn blueberry filling into pie, spreading it out evenly over whipped cream.

Return to refrigerator until serving time. No additional cream will be needed on top of pie.

CRIMSON PIE *Serves 8*

1/2 orange, small, unpeeled, cut into pieces, seeded

4 cups blueberries, washed, dried

3 cups cranberries, washed, picked over

1-1/2 cups sugar

3 tablespoons cornstarch

2 pie crusts

2 tablespoons butter, cut into pieces

For brushing milk

As needed sugar

In blender or processor container, chop orange fine. Transfer to heavy medium saucepan. To saucepan add blueberries, cranberries, sugar, and cornstarch. Mix well. Over medium heat, bring mixture to boil and cook until thick, stirring constantly, about 3 minutes. Cool completely.

Heat oven to 400°F. Roll 1 pie crust out on floured surface; transfer to 9-inch glass pie dish. Gently press into place and trim edges, leaving 1/4-inch overhang. Reserve trimmings.

Spoon berry filling into crust, mounding slightly in center. Dot filling with butter.

Roll out second pie crust. Cover pie filling. Trim edges, pinch edges together to seal, and crimp decoratively. Make several slashes in top crust to allow steam to escape. Brush crust with milk.

Gather trimmings and roll out. Cut out decorative leaves and press gently on top of pie in center. Brush leaves with milk. Sprinkle top of pie with sugar. Place pie on rimmed cookie sheet and bake until crust is golden brown, about 50 minutes. Cool on rack 1 hour. Serve warm or at room temperature.

STEAMED BLUEBERRY PUFF

2 cups flour

2 teaspoons baking powder

1 teaspoon salt

1-1/2 cups milk

As desired blueberries, washed, dried

Into a medium bowl sift flour, baking powder and salt; Mix. Add milk; mix well. Batter will be soft.

Butter individual molds and place them on a steamer rack. Place a spoonful of batter, then a spoonful of blueberries in each mold, alternately until 2/3 full.

Steam 25 minutes. Remove from molds and serve with Blueberry Sauce.

BLUEBERRY SAUCE

4 cups blueberries

1 cup water

1/2 teaspoon lemon zest

1 cup sugar

1 tablespoon cornstarch dissolved in water

In a medium saucepan combine all ingredients. Bring to boil, stirring gently. Lower heat and cook for about 5 minutes, until sauce thickens. Serve warm or cold.

SOUR CREAM BLUEBERRY PIE *Serves 8 to 10*

Crust

1-3/4 cups flour

1/4 cup sugar

1 teaspoon cinnamon, ground

1 teaspoon butter

As needed apple cider or water

Filling

8 ounces sour cream

3 ounces cream cheese

1 egg, large

3/4 cup brown sugar, dark

1/4 cup flour

1 teaspoon vanilla

1 egg white, beaten

2 pints blueberries, washed, dried

If desired Walnut Crumb Topping or whipped cream

Heat oven to 450°F.

Crust

In a medium bowl, combine flour, sugar, cinnamon, and salt. Cut in butter with pastry blender until consistency of coarse meal. Add just enough apple cider to moisten pastry mixture evenly. About 2 tablespoons will be needed. Press dough into ball. Roll out on lightly floured board. Turn pastry into a deep dish 9- or 10-inch pie pan. Flute edges to make a thick raised rim.

Filling

In a medium bowl, combine sour cream, cream cheese, egg, brown sugar, flour, and vanilla. Mix until well combined.

With beaten white, brush pastry crust. Fill pie shell with blueberries. Pour cream mixture over berries.

Bake for 10 minutes at 450°F; reduce temperature to 350°F and bake 35 to 40 minutes more if finishing with Walnut Crumb Topping. If using whipped cream, bake 50 minutes.

If using Walnut Crumb Topping, remove pie from oven, add topping mixture evenly over pie and return to oven for 10 to 15 minutes. Let pie cool on rack before slicing. If desired garnish pie with whipped cream and additional blueberries.

Walnut Crumb Topping

1 cup walnuts, chopped fine

1/2 cup flour

1/2 cup sugar

1/2 cup brown sugar, dark

1/4 teaspoon salt

1 tablespoon cinnamon, ground

1/4 pound butter

In a medium bowl, combine walnuts, flour, sugars, cinnamon, and salt. Mix well. Add butter and mix until crumbly. Use for topping pie, adding to pie for last 10 to 15 minutes of baking time.

BLUEBERRY TART   *Serves 8*

1/4 cup almonds, chopped fine

1/3 cup sugar

2 tablespoons flour

1 tart shell, unbaked

4 cups blueberries, washed, dried

1 tablespoon confectioners' sugar

For topping sour cream, sweetened or vanilla ice cream

Heat oven to 425°F.

In a medium bowl, combine almonds, 2 tablespoons sugar, and flour; mix well. Sprinkle mixture evenly into tart shell. Spread blueberries over almond mixture. Sprinkle berries with remaining 1 tablespoon plus 1 teaspoon sugar.

Place tart on bottom rack of oven, reduce temperature to 400°F, and bake for about 45 minutes, or until crust is golden brown. Transfer tart to rack to cool completely.

Before serving, dust with confectioners sugar. Serve in wedges accompanied with sweetened sour cream or vanilla ice cream.

Tart Shell   *Makes one 11-1/2 inch shell*

1-1/2 cups flour

1 stick plus 4 tablespoons butter, unsalted cold,cut into small pieces, frozen

1 tablespoon sugar

Pinch salt

3 to 4 tablespoons water, ice cold

In a bowl combine flour, butter, sugar, and salt. Mix until coarse crumbs form. Sprinkle ice water over crumbs and mix until well combined. Transfer to work surface. Knead crumbs into a cohesive dough. Use a bit more water if necessary.

Shape dough into 5-inch disk, wrap in wax paper, and refrigerate for 15 minutes.

Flour work surface. Using floured rolling pin, roll out dough into a 13-inch circle about 1/8-inch thick. Brush off excess flour, fold in quarters, and transfer to tart pan. Unfold and press dough flush with rim. Prick bottom of shell all over with fork. Wrap shell well and place in freezer for at least 1 hour and up to 2 days.

BLUEBERRY CHEESE TART   *Serves 10 to 12*

Crust

1-1/2 cups flour

2 tablespoons sugar

1/4 teaspoon salt

1/4 cup vegetable shortening

1/4 cup butter, cut into cubes

1/4 cup water

1 egg white

Filling

2 8-ounce packages cream cheese

1/2 cup lemon juice, fresh

1 teaspoon lemon peel, grated

1 14-ounce can condensed milk, sweetened

1 teaspoon vanilla extract

Topping

3-1/2 cups blueberries, washed, dried
1/4 cup apple jelly

Heat oven to 400°F.

Crust

In a large bowl, combine flour, sugar, and salt. With pastry blender cut in shortening and butter until mixture resembles coarse crumbs. Sprinkle in water, 1 tablespoon at a time, tossing with fork after each addition until pastry holds together.

Form into a ball, then flatten slightly. Wrap in plastic and refrigerate 1 hour for easier rolling. On lightly floured surface, roll pastry into 13-inch circle. Transfer to tart pan. Prick pastry bottom with fork. Refrigerate 2 hours.

Line pastry shell with foil and add layer of weights (or uncooked beans). Bake 10 minutes. Remove weights and foil. Brush with egg white and bake until golden, about 10 or 12 minutes more. Cool.

Filling

In a small mixing bowl, beat cream cheese until soft. Add lemon juice and peel. Beat until well combined. Add condensed milk and vanilla, beating until well mixed. Pour filling into cooled shell. Refrigerate until firm, at least 2 hours.

Topping

Arrange blueberries on top of filling.

In a small saucepan, melt apple jelly. Brush over blueberries. Refrigerate at least 1 hour before serving.

LEMON-BLUEBERRY TART   *Serves 8*

Lemon Curd

10 tablespoons sugar

4 egg yolks, room temperature

6 tablespoons lemon juice, fresh

1/4 cup butter, cut into pieces

2 teaspoons lemon peel, grated

Tart Shell

1-1/2 cups flour

2 tablespoons sugar

1/4 teaspoon salt

1/4 cup vegetable shortening

1/4 cup butter, cut into small pieces

1/4 cup water

1 egg white, beaten

Blueberry Topping

1/3 cup sugar

1 tablespoon cornstarch

1/2 cup water

1-1/2 teaspoons lemon juice, fresh

3 cups blueberries, washed, dried

Heat oven to 400°F.

Lemon Curd

In heavy non-aluminum saucepan, beat sugar and yolks to blend. Add lemon juice, butter, and salt. Over medium heat cook until mixture thickly coats back of spoon, about 8 minutes; do not boil. Immediately strain into airtight container, pressing with back of spoon to extract as much curd as possible.

Mix in lemon peel; cool. Cover and refrigerate at least 1 hour. (Can be prepared 1 week ahead).

Tart Shell

In large bowl combine flour, sugar, and salt. With pastry blender, cut in shortening and butter until mixture resembles coarse crumbs.

Sprinkle in water 1 tablespoon at a time, tossing with fork after each addition until pastry holds together. Form into a ball, then flatten slightly. Wrap in plastic and refrigerate 1 hour for easier rolling.

On lightly floured surface, roll pastry into a 13-inch circle. Transfer to tart pan. Prick pastry bottom with fork. Refrigerate 2 hour.

Line pastry shell with foil and add a layer of pastry weights (or uncooked beans). Bake 10 minutes. Remove weights and foil. Brush with egg white and bake until golden, about 10 to 12 minutes; cool.

Spread lemon curd in crust. Set aside.

Blueberry Topping

In heavy medium saucepan, combine sugar and cornstarch. Mix in water and lemon juice. Over medium heat, cook mixture, stirring, until thicken and translucent. Mix in blueberries, coating well. Immediately transfer berries to tart, using slotted spoon. Refrigerate at least 30 minutes before serving.

BLUEBERRY COTTAGE PUDDING   *Serves 6*

6 cups blueberries, washed, dried
1/2 cup honey
1 egg, beaten
1 tablespoon cornstarch
1-1/2 cups flour
1/2 cup sugar
2 teaspoons baking powder
1/2 cup milk
1/2 cup butter, melted
1 egg, beaten
Garnish cream, whipped or ice cream

Heat oven to 375°F. Butter an 8x8x2-inch square baking dish. Set aside.

In large bowl, combine blueberries, honey, egg, and corn-starch; mix gently. Transfer to prepared dish.

In medium bowl combine flour, sugar, baking powder, and salt; mix

In a small bowl combine milk, butter, and egg. Mix well and add to dry ingredients; mix until just combined. Spoon over berries, spreading to edges.

Bake in 375°F oven until tester inserted in center comes out clean, about 45 minutes. Serve warm with ice cream or whipped cream.

BLUEBERRY PUDDING   *Serves 8*

1 cup blueberries, washed, dried

1 cup pancake mix

1/3 cup honey

2 tablespoons shortening, melted

1 cup milk

In a large bowl, sprinkle 2 to 3 tablespoons pancake mix over blueberries. Set aside.

In a large bowl, mix together shortening, milk, and honey; add pancake mix and stir lightly. Add blueberries.

In a 5-cup mold, add mixture and steam for 2 hours. Any leftover dough may be used for blueberry pancakes.

BLUEBERRY RICE PUDDING *Serves 6 to 8*

3/4 cup rice, uncooked

6 eggs

1 cup sugar

2 cups milk

1 teaspoon vanilla

1 cup blueberries, washed, dried

Optional cinnamon

Heat oven to 350°F.

In a medium saucepan in salted boiling water, cook rice until almost tender, 15 to 20 minutes. Drain well and allow to cool.

In a medium bowl, lightly beat eggs. Stir in sugar, milk, and vanilla. Stir in cooled rice and gently fold in blueberries. Transfer to baking dish and bake in 350°F oven for 30 to 40 minutes, or until knife inserted in center comes out clean. Serve warm or chilled. Garnish with cinnamon if desired.

BLUEBERRY BREAD PUDDING *Serves 4 to 6*

2 cups bread, torn

1/2 cup butter, melted

4 cups blueberries, washed, dried

1/2 cup brown sugar, light

2 cups milk

6 eggs

2 tablespoons lemon juice, fresh

1/4 teaspoon cinnamon, ground

Heat oven to 350°F.

In a large bowl, crumble bread to form coarse crumbs; mix with melted butter.

Butter a 1 quart casserole and make a layer of crumbs; cover with a layer of berries. Sprinkle berries with part of sugar and lemon juice. Repeat layers and top with a dusting of cinnamon and a bit more brown sugar to taste.

In a medium bowl combine eggs and milk; mix well. Pour over casserole mixture. Top with a dusting of cinnamon.

Bake in 350°F for 45 minutes. Watch that top does not over brown. Place sheet of aluminum foil over pudding, if needed to control browning. Let cool to room temperature and serve with ice cream or whipped cream.

BLUEBERRY BISCUITS   *Serves 6*

4 cups blueberries, washed, dried

3 tablespoons sugar

2 cups flour

2-1/2 teaspoons baking powder

1/2 teaspoon salt

6 tablespoons butter, unsalted, chilled, cut in bits

3/4 cup milk

1 pint cream, heavy
1 tablespoon brandy (or vanilla)
For garnish mint sprigs

Heat oven to 450°F.

In medium bowl, toss berries with 1 tablespoon sugar. Cover and refrigerate for at least 1 hour or up to 4 hours.

In large bowl, stir together flour, baking powder, salt, and remaining 2 tablespoons sugar.

Using pastry blender cut in butter until mixture resembles very coarse meal. With a fork, quickly stir in milk; mix until dough holds together. Transfer dough to floured surface; knead for a few seconds until it forms a ball. Pat dough until 1/2-inch thick.
Using biscuit cutter, cut six 3-inch rounds. Transfer to ungreased cooking sheet. Bake in 450°F for 12 to 15 minutes, or until golden; let cool on a rack.

In medium bowl, beat heavy cream until it thickens slightly, then beat in brandy. To serve, place some thickened cream in center of each dessert plate. Split each biscuit in half and place bottom half on cream. Heap the fruit on biscuit and cap with biscuit top. Garnish with mint sprig, if desired. Pass any remaining cream at table.

SOUR CREAM BLUEBERRY BREAD
Makes one 9-inch loaf

2 cups flour
1 teaspoon baking soda
1/2 teaspoon salt
1/2 teaspoon cinnamon, ground
1 cup butter, softened
3/4 cup sugar
2 eggs, large
2 cup banana, ripe, mashed
1/2 cup sour cream
1 cup blueberries, washed, dried
1/2 cup pecans, chopped coarse

Heat oven to 350°F. Butter and flour one 9x5-inch loaf pan.

On waxed paper, sift together flour, baking soda, salt, and cinnamon.

In large bowl, cream butter and sugar until light and fluffy. Add eggs, bananas, and sour cream; beat until blended. Gradually beat in dry ingredients until smooth. Fold in blueberries and pecans. Spoon batter into prepared pan.

Bake in 350°F for 1 hour, or until golden on top and cake tester inserted in center comes out clean. Let cool completely in pan. This moist loaf stays fresh for days. Great toasted for breakfast.

BLUEBERRY NUT BREAD   *Makes 2 loaves*

1 cup whole wheat flour

2 cups flour

1 cup sugar

1 tablespoon baking powder

1/2 teaspoon baking soda

1/2 teaspoon salt

1/2 teaspoon nutmeg

2 eggs

1 cup applesauce

1/4 cup vegetable oil

2 cups blueberries, washed, dried

1/2 cup nuts, chopped

Heat oven to 350°F. Grease and flour 2 loaf pans. Set aside.

In large bowl, combine flours, sugar, baking powder, baking soda, salt, and nutmeg; mix well.

In medium bowl, beat eggs and mix in applesauce and oil. Add wet ingredients to dry ingredients, stirring just enough to blend. Fold in blueberries and nuts.

Transfer batter to prepared loaf pans. Bake in 350°F oven for 50 minutes, or until a cake tester inserted in center of loaves comes out clean.

Cool in pans on rack for 10 minutes. Remove bread from pans and cool on racks. This is a moist loaf which makes a nice tea bread. It freezes well.

BLUEBERRY LEMON BREAD

Makes one 8-inch loaf

1-1/2 cups flour

1 teaspoon baking powder

1/4 teaspoon salt

6 tablespoons butter, room temperature

1-1/2 cups sugar

2 eggs, large

2 teaspoons lemon peel, grated

1/2 cup milk

1-1/2 cups blueberries, washed, dried

3 tablespoons lemon juice, fresh

Heat oven to 325°F. Butter an 8x4x2-inch loaf pan. Set aside.

In a small bowl combine flour, baking powder, and salt. Set aside.

In large bowl, cream butter and 1 cup sugar until mixture is light and fluffy. Add eggs one at a time, beating well after each addition. Add lemon peel. Combine wet and dry ingredients alternately with milk, beginning and ending with dry ingredients. Fold in blueberries.

Spoon batter into prepared loaf pan. Bake in 325°F oven until golden brown and toothpick inserted in center comes out clean, about 1 hour and 15 minutes.

Meanwhile, in a small saucepan, combine 1/3 cup sugar

and lemon juice; bring to boil, stirring until sugar dissolves. With a toothpick pierce top of hot loaf several times. Pour hot lemon mixture over loaf in pan. Cool 30 minutes in pan on rack. Turn bread out of pan and cool completely on rack.

BLUEBERRY- PINEAPPLE FREEZER BREAD
Makes 3 loaves

3 cups flour

2 teaspoons baking powder

1 teaspoon baking soda

2/3 cup vegetable shortening

1-1/2 cups sugar

4 eggs

1/2 cup milk

1-1/2 teaspoons lemon juice, fresh

1 cup pineapple, crushed, drained

2 cups blueberries, washed, dried

1 cup nuts, chopped

1/2 cup coconut, flaked

Heat oven to 350°F. Butter and flour 3 loaf pans. Set aside.

In medium bowl, combine flour, baking powder, baking soda, and salt. Set aside.

In large bowl, cream shortening; add sugar gradually. Stir in eggs, milk, lemon juice, and pineapple. Beat in dry ingredients. Fold in blueberries, nuts, and coconut.

Transfer batter to prepared loaf pans. Bake in 350°F oven for 55 to 60 minutes, or until tester inserted in center comes out clean. Remove from oven and cool on a rack for 10 minutes; remove from pans and continue cooling on rack. Delicious with cream cheese!

BLUEBERRY SCONES   *Makes 8 scones*

4 cups flour

3 tablespoons sugar

4 teaspoons baking powder

12 teaspoon salt

1/2 teaspoon cream of tartar

1/4 cup butter

1 egg, large

1-1/2 cups cream, half-and-half

1-1/2 cups blueberries, washed, dried

Heat oven to 425°F. Grease a large baking sheet.

In large bowl, combine flour, 2 tablespoons sugar, baking powder, salt, and cream of tartar. With pastry blender, cut in butter until mixture resembles coarse crumbs.

Separate egg, placing egg white in cup and yolk in small bowl. With fork beat egg yolk; stir in cream. Add yolk mixture to dry ingredients and mix lightly with fork until mixture clings together to form a soft dough. Turn dough out onto lightly floured surface and knead gently 5 or 6 times. Gently knead in blueberries.

Divide dough in half. With lightly floured rolling pin, roll out half dough into a 7-inch round. Cut into 4 wedges. Repeat with remaining dough. Place scones, 1 inch apart, on greased baking sheet. Pierce tops with tines of fork. Brush with reserved egg white; sprinkle with remaining sugar.

Bake scones at 425°F for 15 to 18 minutes when using fresh blueberries and about 20 minutes when using frozen berries, or until golden brown. Best served warm.

BLUEBERRY CORN MUFFINS   *Makes 12*

2/3 cup cornmeal

1-1/3 cups flour

3 teaspoons baking powder

1/4 teaspoon salt

1/3 cup maple syrup

1/3 cup butter, melted

2 eggs

1 cup blueberries, washed, dried

Heat oven to 425°F. Grease muffin tins or line with paper cups. Set aside.

In a large bowl, combine dry ingredients; in another bowl combine maple syrup, butter, and eggs. Mix liquids well, then quickly stir into dry ingredients with few strokes. Fold in berries and ladle mixture into muffin tins.

Bake at 425°F for 20 to 25 minutes. Serve hot!

LEMON-BLUEBERRY MUFFINS   *Makes 12*

2 eggs, beaten

1/2 cup sugar

3/4 cup vegetable oil

3 tablespoons lemon juice, fresh

1 teaspoon lemon peel, grated

1 teaspoon baking soda

1/2 teaspoon nutmeg, grated fresh

1/2 teaspoon ginger, ground

1/8 teaspoon salt

3/4 cup blueberries, washed, dried

Heat oven to 350°F. Line 12 cup muffin tin with paper liners. Set aside.

In large bowl, beat eggs and sugar until pale and thick, about 2 minutes. Add oil. Stir in lemon juice and peel.

In another bowl, combine 1 cup flour, baking soda, nutmeg, ginger, and salt. Mix well then add to batter. With remaining flour, dredge blueberries. Fold into batter. Pour batter into prepared pan. Bake until lightly browned, about 25 minutes. Transfer muffins to rack. Serve warm.

BLUEBERRY RICOTTA PANCAKES
Makes about 30, 3-inch pancakes

4 eggs, separated, room temperature

1 cup ricotta cheese

1/3 cup sour cream

1/4 cup sugar

2/3 cup flour

2 teaspoons baking powder

1/8 teaspoon salt

3/4 cup milk

2 cups blueberries, washed, dried

Pinch cream of tartar

In large bowl combine thoroughly, egg yolks, ricotta, sour cream, and sugar. In another bowl, sift flour with baking powder and salt. Stir into yolk mixture until smooth. Mix in milk. Fold in blueberries.

In another bowl, beat egg whites with cream of tartar until stiff but not dry. Gently fold 1/4 of whites into batter; fold in remainder.

On a 375°F griddle brushed with oil, ladle batter by 3 tablespoonfuls. Cook until bubbles begin to appear on surface of pancakes, 2 to 3 minutes. Turn and cook until bottoms are golden brown and pancakes are cooked through, 1 to 1-1/2 minutes. Turn and cook until bottoms are golden brown and pancakes are cooked through, 1 to 1-1/2 minutes. Transfer to heated platter. Repeat with remaining batter.

Serve warm with Blueberry Syrup.

BLUEBERRY SYRUP   *Makes 1-3/4 cups*

2 cups blueberries, washed, dried
1/2 cup sugar
1 teaspoon lemon juice, fresh
1/2 teaspoon vanilla

In a small saucepan, cook 1 cup berries, sugar, water, lemon juice, and vanilla, stirring until sugar dissolves. Increase heat and bring to boil. Reduce heat and simmer until mixture thickens to syrup, stirring occasionally. Add remaining 1 cup blueberries and cook until soft, stirring occasionally, about 5 minutes.

Serve warm. Can be prepared 2 days ahead; reheat before serving. Great on pancakes or ice cream!

BLUEBERRY PANCAKES   *Makes about 10*

1 cup flour

2 tablespoons sugar

2 teaspoons baking powder

1/2 teaspoon salt

1 cup milk

1 tablespoon vegetable oil

1 teaspoon vanilla

2 cups blueberries, washed, dried

Heat griddle to 375°F; grease, if necessary.

In large bowl, combine dry ingredients. In another bowl, combine remaining ingredients except blueberries.

Pour wet ingredients into dry ingredients; stir until just mixed. Fold in blueberries. Using about 1/4 cup batter for each pancake, cook 3 to 5 minutes, or until pancakes are fluffy and full of bubbles. Turn and cook other side.

Serve piping hot with syrup of choice.

BLUEBERRY BUTTERMILK WAFFLES
Makes 4 to 6

1 cup flour
1 cup rolled oats
2 cup cornmeal, yellow
4-1/2 teaspoons baking powder
1-1/2 cups blueberries, washed, dried
1 cup yogurt, plain
2 eggs
3/4 cup butter, melted (or vegetable oil)
1 cup buttermilk
Additional yogurt, plain, for topping
Additional blueberries, washed, dried, for topping

In a large bowl, combine flour, oats, cornmeal, and baking powder; mix well. Add yogurt, eggs, butter, and buttermilk. Blend well. Gently fold in blueberries. Let batter stand 15 minutes before baking.

Heat waffle iron. Pour batter to cover about 2/3 of grid. Bake until steam has stopped and waffles are golden, 3 to 4 minutes.

Serve hot waffles topped with a scoop of yogurt and fresh berries.

BLUEBERRY BUTTERMILK GRIDDLE CAKES
Makes about 12

1 cup flour

2 tablespoons cornmeal

1 tablespoon sugar

1 teaspoon baking powder

1/2 teaspoon baking soda

1/2 teaspoon salt

1/8 teaspoon cinnamon, ground

1 cup buttermilk

1 egg

2 tablespoons butter, melted

1-1/2 cups blueberries, washed, dried

Heat griddle over low heat. In this recipe, blueberries are added to batter after it has been poured on griddle to avoid having griddle cakes turn blue.

In large bowl, whisk together flour, cornmeal, sugar, baking powder, baking soda, salt, and cinnamon

In a small bowl, whisk together the buttermilk, egg, and oil. Pour into dry ingredients; stir lightly until just a few lumps remain. Do not overmix or pancakes will be tough.

Increase heat under griddle. Grease lightly. Ladle about 3 tablespoons batter onto griddle for each pancake. Scatter 2 tablespoons blueberries on top of each. Cook until undersides are golden brown, 2 to 3 minutes. Flip and cook until center springs back when lightly pressed, another 2 to 3 minutes. Repeat with remaining batter.

Serve cakes hot from griddle or keep warm in 200°F oven while cooking the remainder. Serve with butter and maple syrup.

BLUEBERRY-FILLED CREPES   *Serves 4*

1 egg
2 tablespoons flour
3 tablespoons milk

In a large bowl, combine ingredients and beat until well mixed. Set aside for a few minutes.

Spray a 6-inch crepe or omelet pan with cooking spray; heat over medium heat.

Pour 2 tablespoons batter into pan and quickly rotate pan so batter covers pan bottom evenly.

Cook about 30 seconds until surface of pancake dries. Turn and cook the second side a few seconds more.

Turn out onto plate. Continue making crepes, one at a time. Separate crepes with wax paper.

BLUEBERRY FILLING   *Fills 4 crepes*

1 cup blueberries, washed, drained

1/4 cup sour cream, low fat

1/4 cup yogurt, vanilla, low fat

In a small bowl, combine sour cream and yogurt; mix thoroughly.

To assemble crepes, spoon 3 tablespoons berries into center of each crepe; add some yogurt mixture. Roll crepes and arrange on a serving plate. Makes 4 filled crepes.

BLUEBERRY SALAD   *Makes 6 cups*

Fruit

1 avocado, peeled, cubed

1 pint blueberries, washed, dried

1 cantaloupe, medium peeled, cubed

1 tablespoon lime juice, fresh

Dressing   *Makes 1 cup*

1 cup sour cream

1 tablespoon sugar

1 tablespoon lime juice

2 tablespoons mint, fresh, minced

      (or 1 teaspoon mint, dried, crumbled)

In small bowl, combine dressing ingredients and mix well. Set aside.

In medium bowl, toss avocado with lime juice. Add blueberries and cantaloupe; toss gently.

Serve fruit topped with dressing.

COLD BLUEBERRY SOUP   *Serves 6*

1 pint blueberries, washed, dried

1-1/2 cups water

1/4 cup sugar

1 3-inch strip lemon peel

1 2-inch stick cinnamon

3/4 cup sour cream

In medium saucepan, combine blueberries, water, sugar, lemon peel, and cinnamon stick. Over medium heat bring to boil; simmer 15 minutes. Cool 10 minutes; remove lemon and cinnamon. Pour into blender container; cover and puree. Chill at least 4 hours, or overnight. Just before serving, stir in sour cream. Delicious as a beginning or ending to summer dinner.

RED WINE BLUEBERRY SOUP *Serves 6*

1 cup blueberries

1/2 cup water

1/4 cup sugar

1/2 cup lemon juice, fresh

1 teaspoon coriander, ground

1/4 teaspoon cinnamon, ground

1/2 cup yogurt, plain

1/2 cup sour cream

1/2 cup red wine, dry

In blender, puree blueberries until smooth.

In medium saucepan, combine blueberry puree, water, sugar, lemon juice, and spices. Over low heat, simmer for 10 minutes.

Whisk in remaining ingredients, blending until smooth. Chill for several hours before serving.

BLUEBERRY HONEY SAUCE *Makes about 1-1/2 cups*

2 cups blueberries, washed, dried

1 teaspoon cinnamon, ground

1/2 teaspoon nutmeg, grated fresh

1/2 cup honey

1/4 cup butter, unsalted

Pinch salt

In medium saucepan, combine blueberries, cinnamon, nutmeg, honey, butter, and salt; bring mixture to boil, stirring occasionally. Simmer, stirring occasionally, for 5 minutes.

Serve sauce warm over ice cream, waffles, or pancakes.

BLUEBERRY CHAMBORD SAUCE
Makes about 2 cups

3/4 cup water
1/4 cup sugar
2 teaspoons cornstarch
2 teaspoons lemon juice, fresh
1 cup blueberries, washed, dried
1 teaspoon butter
1/2 teaspoon cinnamon, ground
1 teaspoon orange peel, grated
1 tablespoon chambord liqueur

In medium saucepan, combine water, sugar, and cornstarch; whisk.

Add lemon juice and over medium heat, bring to a boil.

Add blueberries and cook about 2 minutes. Remove from heat; add butter, cinnamon, and Chambord liqueur. Stir until butter is dissolved and incorporated.

Serve warm over vanilla ice cream, waffles, pancakes, or pound cake.

BLUEBERRY CHUTNEY   *Makes about 4 cups*

7 cups blueberries, washed, dried

1-1/2 cups red wine vinegar

1 onion, medium, peeled, minced

1/2 cup raisins, golden

1/2 cup brown sugar, light, packed tight

2 teaspoons yellow mustard seed

1 tablespoon ginger, crystallized, grated

1/2 teaspoon cinnamon, ground

Pinch salt

Pinch nutmeg, ground

Pinch coriander, ground

1/2 teaspoon red pepper, dried, crushed

In a large saucepan, place blueberries and crush lightly with wooden spoon.

Add remaining ingredients; over medium heat, bring to boil, stirring often.

Boil steadily, stirring occasionally, for about 45 minutes. Chutney will be thick.

Spoon into hot, sterilized half-pint jars and seal. Store for 1 month or so before serving. Refrigerate after opening jar.

BLUEBERRY-APPLE CONSERVE   *Makes 6-1/2 pints*

4 cups blueberries, washed, dried

4 medium apples, tart, cored, peeled, chopped

6 cups sugar

1/2 cup raisins, yellow

1/4 cup lemon juice, fresh

1/2 cup pecans, chopped

In a large saucepan over medium heat, combine blueberries, apples, sugar, raisins, and lemon juice; bring to boil, stirring occasionally, until sugar dissolves.
Cook rapidly until thick, stirring often. Add pecans.

Pour hot conserve into hot sterilized 2-pint jars. Adjust caps. Cool and store in a cool, dark place. After opening jar, store in refrigerator.

BLUEBERRY-CITRUS JAM   *Makes 6 2-pints*

1 lemon

1 orange

1 cup water

4 cups blueberries, washed, dried

5-1/2 cups sugar

1 box fruit pectin

Chop lemon and orange into large chunks; remove seeds. In food chopper, chop coarse. Save juice.

To a large nonaluminum pot, transfer fruit and juices. Add water and bring to boil. Cover and simmer for 10 minutes.

In a large bowl, crush blueberries; add to cooked orange and lemon. Simmer for another 10 minutes. Add sugar and stir until sugar dissolves. Bring to a full rolling boil. Allow to boil hard for 1 minute. Stir constantly to prevent sticking. Remove from heat and stir in pectin. Stir and skim off foam.

Ladle into hot sterilized jars. Seal with paraffin and let cool. Wipe off jars; store in a dark cool place. After opening jar, store in refrigerator.

BLUEBERRY-SHALLOT MARMALADE
Makes about 1 cup

3 shallots, large, peeled, sliced thin

1 tablespoon vegetable oil

1 cup brown sugar, light, packed

1/2 cup raspberry vinegar

1/4 cup red wine, dry

1 sprig thyme, fresh

1 quart blueberries, washed, dried

1 small bay leaf

In a large fry pan in oil, saute shallot until lightly golden; set aside.

In a medium pot, heat sugar until it melts. Add vinegar, wine, and shallots (mixture will separate), stirring well.

Add blueberries and herbs; simmer until volume is reduced by half.
Cool to room temperature, or refrigerate but allow to come to room temperature before serving.

BLUEBERRY JAM   *Makes 6 jars*
20 cups blueberries, washed, dried
2 4-inch sticks cinnamon
3 green apples, chopped fine
1 orange, rind grated
1 cup honey (or to taste)
1 lemon, juice of
1 tablespoon vanilla

In a large pot, place blueberries; add 1 to 2 cups water. Over medium heat, bring to boil, then add cinnamon sticks, apple, and orange rind. Simmer, uncovered, 20 minutes, stirring frequently. Add honey and cook over low heat an additional 30 minutes, stirring often. Remove cinnamon stick and add lemon juice and vanilla. Mix well.

Pour mixture into sterilized jars, leaving 1/4-inch headroom. Seal with melted paraffin and cool. Store in a cool dark place. After opening jar, store in refrigerator.

BLUEBERRY VINEGAR   *Makes 3 cups*

1/2 cup blueberries, washed, dried

2 1-inch sticks cinnamon

2 cups white vinegar

1 tablespoon honey

In a sterilized bottle, place blueberries and cinnamon. Set aside.

In medium saucepan over low heat, heat vinegar and honey; bring to a simmer and cook for 2 minutes. Pour into bottle, cap tightly, and store in a cool, dark place. Let stand at least 2 weeks before using.

BLUEBERRY WINE PUNCH   *Makes about 4 cups*

4 cups blueberries, washed, dried

3 cups rhine wine

3 tablespoons lemon juice, fresh

1/2 cup sugar, superfine granulated (or to taste)

1 cup water, ice cold

In a blender or food processor container, puree 2 cups of blueberries with 1 cup ice water; strain mixture through very fine sieve.

In a pitcher, combine blueberry juice, wine, lemon juice, sugar, and 1 cup crushed ice.

BLUEBERRY CORDIAL   *Makes 3 cups*

3 cups blueberries, washed, dried

1 cup sugar

2 cups vodka

Rinse a 2-quart jar well with boiling water; drain.

In jar, combine blueberries, sugar, and vodka. Seal jar tightly and store in a cool, dark place, shaking jar occasionally, for 2 months.

Strain liquid through very fine sieve lined with triple thickness of rinsed, squeezed cheesecloth into a bowl. Transfer to a decanter.

Serve cordial as an after dinner drink or with tonic over ice as a cocktail.

INDEX

About the Author:

R. Marilyn Schmidt is the author of almost 70 books. She has spent many years researching the New Jersey Pine Barrens. She painstakingly took on the task of clearing the title for Buzby's Chatsworth General Store, located in Chatsworth, New Jersey (the heart of the Pine Barrens) and then renovating the store back to its original condition as much as possible. The store has once again become a meeting place for those interested in the culture and history of the Pine Barrens.

Area residents consider Marilyn to be "an adopted Piney," a title bestowed on precious few folks. It is the title she wears most proudly, although in her lifetime she has claimed many other hats: in addition to being a certified tax assessor and author, she has worked as a biochemist and a pharmacologist. She has a real estate license and has done pottery and painting in her "spare time." It is the latter she hopes to return to when she retires.

Other Fine Titles by R. Marilyn Schmidt:

Cookbooklets for every type of fish, sure to answer the question: What's for dinner tonight? If you love fish but are tired of the same way of cooking it, these cookbooklets will delight your palate.

Blackfish / Tautog	Scallops
Blue Crab	Sea Bass
Caviar	Seafood Chowders, Soups & Bisques
Cod & Pollock	Seafood Salads
Eastern Oysters	Seafood Stir Fry
Flounder & Other Flat Fish	Shad Shad Roe
Hard Shell Clams	Shrimp
Lobsters, North American	Soft Shell Clams
Mackerel, Atlantic/Spanish	Squid
Mahi-Mahi	Sturgeon
Mako Shark	Tilefish
Monkfish	Tilipia / St. Peter's Fish
Mussels	Tuna
Orange Roughy	Weakfish / SeaTrout
Salmon	

A Sampler of Canned Seafood

Here's your answer to serving unexpected or expected guests a gourmet meal! From your pantry you can serve appetizers, salads and entrees from a wide variety of canned seafood: anchovies, clams, conch, crab, herring, lobster, mackerel, oysters, salmon, sardines, shrimp, and of course, tuna. Learn the best ways for handling canned seafood.

Bargain Seafoods

Bargain seafood, sometimes called "trash fish" are those in abundance and sometimes discarded by fisherman. These seafood are underappreciated. Wonderful flavors and economical prices await you. Try Atlantic Mackerel, Atlantic Pollock, Butterfish, Croaker, Cusk, Dogfish, Eel, Ling or Red Hake, Mussels, Sea Robins, Sharks, Skates and Rays, Smelts, and Whiting or Silver Lake. All are delicious!

Chutney Complete

Chutneys, easy to make, versatile, and distinctive, preserve fresh vegetables and fruit for year round use. Making chutney is almost foolproof, not like jellies and jams. Chutneys make great gifts. Serve with meats, cheeses, or just on crackers.

Cooking the Shore Catch

New Jersey's seafood at its finest! Traditional recipes for both finfish and shellfish from Sandy Hook to Cape May enable you to cook everyone's favorites. Recipes from fisherman and their wives, some long gone and those here today. A must for those who "go down the shore." Recipes are for seafood caught commonly in New Jersey's waters.

Flavored Vinegars

Flavored vinegars are an "in" product. Easy to make, great to use. Here are directions for making over 32 different vinegars and vinaigrettes. Give a unique gift of your own special vinegar. Use the extra herbs from your garden.

Herb Sauces, Salsas, and Such

Tired of paying high prices for seasonings and sauces? Make your own! Here are recipes for 75 herb-flavored condiments. Perfect for gifts, delicious to taste, and inexpensive to make. Use your own herb crop for a top quality product.

How to Write a Family Cookbook

Ever wonder how your grandmother made that fantastic stew? Do your kids ask for favorite family recipes? Why not preserve these favorites for future generations? This booklet gives briefly the "how to" of writing and publishing your family cookbook. This is a perfect gift for family and friends.

Mustard Magic

Grow your own mustard plants and make mustards from your crop, or from purchased dry mustard and seeds. Recipes are included for making 32 mustards and 15 mustard sauces and dressings. Try making your own special mustard. Great gifts!

Seafood Secrets:
A Nutritional Guide to Seafood

We live in a health conscious era. Daily we are bombarded by articles on weight control, heart disease, diet and drugs. Diet is important – essentially, you are what you eat! Recently, seafood has been emphasized as "heart food." Why? Research data confirms that increased fish consumption leads to reduced risk of heart disease. There are often questions concerning whether a particular fish or shellfish is allowed on our specific diet. Often questions arise such as "Can I eat scallops when I have to watch my cholesterol level?" or "Is saltwater fish too high in salt for my low salt diet?" This book supplies you with the answers to these questions and the basic information needed to guide you in the selection of seafood for your special dietary needs. Cooking and health hints will guide you in how to reduce the calories in your favorite recipes.

Seafood Smoking, Grilling, Barbecuing

Use your grill to cook an entire meal! Here are recipes for finfish and shellfish plus recipes for sauces and directions for grilling fruits and vegetables, too. Just think, no pans to wash. Your entire dinner is on the grill.

All titles can be purchased on line at: www.pinebarrenspress.com. Most of the books can also be purchased at Amazon, both in paperback and for Kindle.

Wholesale prices are also available for bulk quantities. Please call 609.758.1304 or send an email to info@kfrcommunications. com for more information.

Made in the USA
Charleston, SC
04 March 2012